Naturally Psychic

A world of self-discovery

Gypsy Maggie Rose

Naturally Psychic

A world of self-discovery

Gypsy Maggie Rose
2024

Published by Margaret Rose Sinton, 2024.

Copyright © 2024

Margaret Rose Sinton. All rights reserved.

All rights reserved. Except for short extracts for review, no part of this book is to be reproduced, stored in a retrieval system, or transmitted in any form or by any means without the publisher and copyright owner's prior written permission.

ISBN: 978-0-646-89625-0

First edition.

Dedication

*For John, my husband,
my friend, my support,
for always having my back,
for trusting in my dreams,
and for allowing me to fly free.*

Contents

Foreword 1
Preface 5
Introduction 7
   Yes, you are psychic! 7
Housekeeping 13
   Yes, you are psychic! 13
   Processes 15
   Light protection 16
   Breath 17
   Centred breath 18
   Belly breath 19
   Alternate nostril breathing 21
Chapter One – The Gift of Knowing 23
   Knowing is the most future-based of all the senses 24
   As you think so, shall you be 25
      Exercise - Knowing 30
Chapter Two – The Gift of Seeing 31
   To see 32
   Higher sight 34
   Sunrise and sunset 35
   Extended vision 36
   Vision versus seeing 38
      Group exercise – Seeing 39
      Single person exercise – Seeing 39
Chapter Three – The Gift of Hearing 41
   Eating the sun 42

- The wind 47
- Working with the wind 48
- Archangels and the wind 48
- Calling the Archangels 50
- Ways to boost your psychic senses 51
- The heart 53

Chapter Four – The Gift of Feeling 55
- What are the hallmarks of a person high in feeling? 57
- How does it feel? 58
- Where is the feeling centre located? 59
- How to activate the feeling centre 60
- Belly breathing 61
  - Exercise – Feeling 61
- How can feeling help you? 63
  - Added extra belly button joy 64
- Your body does not lie 65
- Pain control 65
  - Exercise – Feeling (in pain control) 65
  - Exercise – Feeling 67
  - Exercise – Feeling 69
  - Exercise – Feeling 69
- Sensing spirit 71
  - Cold spots 71
  - Hot spots 71
  - Rapping, scratching, knocking 72
  - Energy drains and equipment malfunctions 72
  - Physical sensations 73
  - Smells 73
  - Tastes 73
  - Mists and other masses 74
  - Apparitions 74

- Disembodied voices 74
- Orbs and light anomalies 74
- Aura 75
- People watching 76
- Silence 77
- Reaching silence 78
- Metaphysical aids 80
- The singing stick 83
- Ouija board 85
- Stepping into spirit 86
- Chapter Five – Psychic Ability and Spirituality 91
- But how? 93
- Chapter Six – Chakra System 95
- What is the chakra system? 96
  - Root Chakra 96
  - Sacral Chakra 96
  - Solar Plexus Chakra 97
  - Heart Chakra 97
  - Throat Chakra 97
  - Third Eye Chakra 97
  - Crown Chakra 97
- Sensing Chakra energies 98
- Chapter Seven – Infinity Breathing 103
- Acknowledgments 111
- About the Author 107
- News and Media 111
- Testimonials 115
- Connect with Maggie 117

Foreword

I had the great privilege of connecting with Maggie well over a decade ago. When we met, instantly, it was as if I had known her my whole life. Maggie has taught me many things, and I'm quite sure that she is completely unaware of the incredible impact she has on all those she connects with.

Maggie is a natural born healer, teacher, guide, mentor and of course, she is a gifted psychic medium as well as an honest and inspiring writer, storyteller and author.

If you are lucky enough to share Maggie's world, you will soon realise that she sees things in the deepest of colours where it's often the case that most of us spend our whole lives only viewing the world in black and white.

Gypsy Maggie Rose

I remember a day we spent together, exploring the incredible waterfalls, mountains and vastness that is found in my hometown—Far North Queensland.

The gratitude that Maggie had for everything she witnessed that day was inspiring. Her appreciation for the physical world and its awe and beauty transcends far beyond what most of us can fully understand. She sees what most of us cannot and when you combine this gift with her many other gifts of wisdom and insight, it is this mix that makes Maggie such an incredible teacher and healer.

If you are lucky enough to open one of Maggie's books, you will soon feel the love and wisdom pouring from every page. And if you are ready to receive her insight and knowledge, well, it's a good idea to prepare yourself, because she will gift you with more AHA moments than you can ever imagine.

I believe that there are no coincidences in life and so, if you have found yourself here and feel somehow connected to this book, Naturally Psychic, then turn the page. When you open yourself up to Maggie's world and her teachings, your life will be changed forever.

Jo Ettles
Published Author

Published books
The Shed, Underneath My Clothes, Project Shine

As seen in
The Huffington Post, Deepak Chopra's CHOPRA, MEDIUM, Tiny Buddha, That's Life, Mind Body Green and Motivation Grid.

Preface

Welcome to the wonderful world of self-discovery and a splash of gypsy magic

Many of us see psychics as a privileged few with a special gift.

Myth and mystery surround it, making it even more exciting and unattainable—rubbish, absolute rubbish.

I do not deny that there are many advanced souls among us who have activated their abilities or had the good fortune to grow up in surroundings that supported their spiritual growth.

Many ask if a psychic ability is spiritual. The answer is yes and no.

When you tap into your psychic ability, you can enhance your experience of spirituality.

However, here it comes, so get ready for a shock.

Psychic ability and psychic centres are located within the physical body.

Yes, you read that correctly. Psychic centres are within the physical body of every living soul.

So, enjoy the journey because you are included.

Introduction

Yes, you are psychic!

The fact of the matter is that each of us is born psychic. So, yes, you can learn to stretch and wake up your psychic abilities to reach higher levels of understanding about who and what you are.

Psychic ability is not only normal—it is your birthright. Each of us uses our psychic energies in our day-to-day lives. It is simply a matter of developing the muscles.

We have five physical senses: taste, touch, hearing, seeing and smell.

We also have four psychic senses: knowing, seeing, hearing and feeling.

This is, in reality, normal, and it takes a little time to get your head around it. But then so did learning to walk and talk and the million other things we do on an automatic level, no questions asked.

Try to understand that this is normality, but who wants to be normal? Not me and no one will tell me what to do.

We have also accepted the story that some *gifted* people have access to the magical, elusive sixth sense. Fortunately, with many beings awakening to the true purpose of life, questions are being asked.

When I do readings for others, I am constantly asked questions. *Am I psychic? What is my gift, if indeed there is one?* This book describes that not only are there nine senses, but they are already in action in your day-to-day life.

Then we will learn. We will learn how to locate and activate the nine senses *on command*. We will learn to tune into that elusive psychic part of our reality.

What are these mysterious extras?

They are knowing, seeing, hearing and feeling. We may know these by names like clairvoyant, clairsentient, empathy and many others.

This book is essentially a step-by-step course I keep simple and relatable. We are halfway there if you can accept the extra senses are normal.

We need to view these senses as unused muscles. Use a muscle, and it becomes stronger and stronger. Neglect the same muscle, and it shrinks and becomes painful to deal with.

Most of us have not had training in exercising these psychic muscles. They have likely shrunk and could be painful to activate. Equally, they might activate slowly or have been ready for a while. It is all about starting the process and moving towards their activation.

Remember, the more you put in, the more you get back.

So, where do these *psychic muscles* sit in the body?

To understand where these muscles sit, we need to know that our physical and psychic senses respond to energy and vibrational patterns.

Everything around us is energy in motion or a vibrational pattern. The higher the energy output, the higher the vibration.

We know emotion activates energy and can set a huge process in motion. Whether you stretch to wake up in the morning, practice a yoga pose, or stretch clairvoyant muscles, they all begin the same way. There is the intention, the stretch and the connection.

Just because we do not understand how something works does not mean the process does not work. We may not be aeronautical scientists, but we accept we get on a plane to fly somewhere, and the process works. Most people accept the reality without questioning its origins.

We are unaware of the electrical currents and energy transformations that occur during our day-to-day activities, including thoughts, walking, sleeping and eating.

We are also unaware of the workings of the psychic centres. They just do their thing. Locating the psychic centres is easier than you think. This is because they lie within the physical body and are activated by our nervous systems.

Some areas have many nerves, all acting like an electric circuit. These psychic areas are:

- knowing—the crown and top of the head
- vision—behind the eyes and upward
- hearing—the head area above the ears
- feeling—the front of the body, breastbone to below the navel.

The navel area is especially significant, as we will discover.

Each of these centres corresponds to massive nerve centres. Nerve centres do an incredible job of relaying information to the brain, which relays the knowledge to where it is needed. They go about their business day in and day out, and we are unaware of the enormous jobs happening within our bodies.

I won't get into the scientific or medical details because they overwhelm me and will probably be too much for you. However, we need to know the locations and activation process of the centres. So, step up and accept the challenge. Ask yourself, what have I got to lose? What have I got to gain? How can these extra abilities help in my day-to-day life?

You and only you hold the key to your physical and psychic well-being. Take control of who and what you are—because you can—and do not allow fear or conditioning to hold you back.

You got this. Let's do it!

Housekeeping

Yes, you are psychic!

There is nothing to fear in flexing your psychic muscles, although you may feel more comfortable adding some protection. This could include crystals, candles, music or incense. This is your life and your way.

We are all painfully aware of the constant barrage of energy from others, leaving those with exceptional sensitivity utterly drained. We all know or have experienced people who *suck us dry*.

This energy overload is more prominent today than ever, with increased populations in the larger cities. We move around more socially in shopping centres, movie theatres and events. Get the picture?

Take a moment to imagine the following *scene*. You have showered, dressed, relaxed, ready for a day of shopping, feeling fresh and alive. A few hours later, you drag yourself in the door laden with packages, feeling like you are carrying the weight of the world.

You found some great bargains and had an incredible catch-up with friends. Still, your feet hurt, your back screams, and your mind is fuzzy. Welcome to energy overload.

Let's establish a clear image of the energetic events that have transpired. Think of a bee leaving the hive, fresh light, buzzing away, happy and free. A few hours later, the same bee staggers into the hive loaded with pollen. You can see the load the bee is carrying. Like you, I am sure the bee enjoyed their day, flitting from flower to flower, gathering the delectable pollen. However, the load is hard to carry.

You are like that bee. Only your *pollen* is energy and is invisible. Unlike you, the bee heads in and unloads every speck of pollen. You are unaware of the load you have picked up. Now, this is where I feel the need for protection needs to be addressed.

Before we start, let's clean up and eliminate the rubbish, as some energy isn't worth it. The issue is that the aura, our extended energy, doesn't distinguish between good and bad; energy is energy. So, we need to accept responsibility to keep our house clean.

Processes

If you have processes that work for you, fantastic, keep working with them. But it never hurts and adds to the repertoire. Let me share with you one of my favourite processes.

Most of us have heard of *white light*. Let me introduce you to the *gypsy* energies of pure *gold and electric blue. Gold* is the colour of cleansing and empowerment. *Electric blue* is the colour of healing. These are the colour vibrations used by the ancients and known to my people for centuries.

Many years ago, I developed a blending of knowledge that gifted me with the following clearing and protection systems. From a physical perspective, it is the spinal cord's bone marrow that serves as the body's central connection. Clearing from the centre reveals the core of things.

If you have read this far, you are ready to be enlightened and to learn about gypsy energies.

Make any of the following processes into a recording or whatever works for you.

Light protection

Take a few moments to relax, put on music, incense, or whatever works for you. Remember one thing: it does not matter what anyone says you *need* to use. This is your experience, your time, your space, your choice. If you have not done this before, try to use your imagination and practice this regularly.

Process

Close your eyes, take some long, deep breaths, and allow yourself to relax and release.

In your mind's eye, see, know, and feel a brilliant golden globe of light hovering above your head. Allow yourself to feel the warmth that emanates from it, and gently allow this light to enter the top of your head.

Gently allow the light to float throughout the head, clearing any unwanted junk energies. Take the time to thoroughly clear around the brain, eyes and throat.

Continue allowing the energy to flow and enter the spinal cord at the base of the skull. Now, gently allow this pure golden energy to flow, vertebrae by vertebrae, down the centre of your spine. Slowly, gently, step-by-step.

Now allow this golden energy to flow from your body down into the Earth.

Repeat this process using the powerful *electric blue* energies until you are like a bead on a golden and blue thread.

Now, the magic begins.

Take a long, slow, deep breath through both nostrils. Release the out breath through the mouth, a long, slow sigh.

Imagining, seeing, feeling, or knowing allows the energies of the combined lights to expand outwards. With each breath out, the circle of light expands outwards until it sits well beyond the body.

After you have finished, you can continue your day or, if in the evening, go to bed.

Nothing needs to be closed or cleared; it has been done. You are in a tube of protection.

The sharing of energy is a gift, so be my guest and pass it on to others.

Breath

The process of breathing may sound like it's a bit on the weird side. After all, we do it naturally. If we didn't, we would have a problem. Yes, it is a natural part of who we are. However, the gift of working with breath to tune into our innate psychic abilities exists.

Have you not noticed how your breath changes because of circumstances? How it catches in your heart and throat when emotions overflow, or with that amazing or not-so-amazing first kiss?

How does it tighten in your throat and hold you speechless in moments of fear or when you are called into the boss's office? How does that scream of pure joy and occasional trepidation erupt from within you on a roller coaster or some other incredible event?

The breath is an amazing barometer that expands the experience. So, it is in the expansion and experience of our psychic energy centres.

Let's look at a few methods of working with the breath that enable this activation to wake up our energy centres and add to the experience daily. Finding methods that make you feel at ease and satisfied is fantastic.

It is my experience that learning never stops. However, if something does not work for you, move on. Remember, different things work for different people.

Centred breath

Balance and harmony are essential in this wild world we live in. Personally, I find the need to grab a few calming moments throughout my rushed day. This process is straightforward and uncomplicated.

Process

Take time out to sit and relax.

Take a deep breath in through both nostrils.

Hold for one or two seconds.

Exhale gently through pursed lips, like giving a kiss.

Repeat until you achieve a sense of calm and regain control.

Try not to focus on any issues. Just breathe.

How easy is that?

I promise you the benefits increase with use, and later, you will find out how to use this centred breath technique to activate a psychic centre.

Belly breath

The belly button or umbilical cord is a much-overlooked energy centre. It gifted us life through the body of our mothers and links us still to our matriarchal lineage and, ultimately, to Mother Earth.

We each retain a significant part of the umbilical cord, which has folded within and holds the key to releasing psychic energies.

Relax and prepare a space to work with this breath, as it can be incredibly energising and open doors to amazing self-discovery. It is also an important process in activating a psychic energy centre.

Process

Take slow, sipping breaths down into the belly. Purse your lips like a kiss. Then sip in the air, sip by sip, like a straw.

Take the sips down to the belly button when you have enough breath. Focus on the belly button for a few seconds.

Release gently through the mouth. Take a few *normal* breaths and start again. This one takes a bit of practice but is worthwhile.

You may like to add to the experience by placing a crystal on your belly button. Crystals you could use are rose quartz to expand love, amethyst for healing, obsidian for protection. Experiment with these crystals and enjoy.

You may also wish to use essential oil to assist and expand your experience. As the Vagus Nerve does its thing best from this area, the addition of the oil supercharges the action. *Be sure* to use only *one drop,* either of a single oil or a blend. It is also best to dilute the essential oil in a carrier oil. Some of the carrier oils have their own healing energies and include sweet almond, avocado, or good old castor oil. My personal favourite is hemp oil.

To use the essential oil, gently massage the oil deeply into the entire area while practising the breathing process. Relax and enjoy the experience while tuning into the body's responses. You may like to try lavender or chamomile for restful sleep, juniper to assist weight loss via releasing water retention, and ylang ylang to connect with your sensual self. The choice is yours.

Alternate nostril breathing

This one can take a little getting used to. However, you will soon settle into a rhythm, which will be great. Sometimes, we are fuzzy or not quite in the flow of things. Now, instead of reaching for a caffeine hit, try this technique. Mind you, sipping coffee is way cooler than playing with your nose, but you'll learn to understand.

Process

Take a few deep breaths and get ready for the fun bit.

Place your left thumb and forefinger on either side of your nostrils.

Close the left nostril with your thumb. Breathe in through the right nostril.

Flip the forefinger to close the right nostril. Breathe out through the left nostril. Breathe in through the left nostril.

Flip the thumb to close the left nostril. Breathe out through the right nostril.

And repeat.

Yes, it takes a bit of practice, but it clears the head and adds that extra boost to keep you going, as well as activating a massive psychic hit.

Now, I do not want to overwhelm you with what may appear as hard work. Trust me, this is about as tough as it gets, so we will move on.

Later, we will discuss the granddaddy of all breath processes, but for now, let's get on with the fun stuff.

Chapter One – The Gift of Knowing

The *gift of knowing* is often called prophecy. A prophecy is equal to intuition. The *gift of knowing* or *psychic intuition* resembles the instantaneous *knowing* that has been the hallmark of prophecy for centuries.

The prophets of old knew it and completely trusted that knowledge. It was the gift of shamans to their people or tribe. In times past, they often taught the spiritual elders, from birth, to work with the psychic realms and to connect with their *other selves*.

This was essential, as the work of most of the tribes was connected to pure survival, hunting for food and finding shelter. Today, we still need to connect to the physical survival of the family.

However, we have so much more leisure time in which we can connect to the inner being. I have often wondered about that statement. Inner being, go within. Well, hello, of course, you would go within yourself, to where the answers lie, within your psychic receptors.

Knowing is the most future-based of all the senses

We *know* things. We know how a situation will turn out. We know if there are going to be issues. It is a deep inside knowing.

Have you ever *just known* something? Have you ever *just known* when someone was going to call? Have you been thinking of someone, and hey presto, they turn up somehow? Have you met someone and known they differed from how they appeared?

If you have, fantastic. You are working with the psychic sense of *knowing*. How easy is that? Yes, I understand this is a grey area for some and a shining light for others. Easy, take baby steps to locate and activate. Locating and activating will become our mantra while we explore these exciting areas.

Think of a baby's excitement and joy as they discover their toes. It is a full-on, fun-filled experience. The joy radiates from them. This is the joy of discovery, and so it is with the journey of the psychic senses. Joy and discovery are the *wow* factors.

It is important to remember that each of us has our own psychic footprint, and we can only walk to the beat of our own drum. So, be gentle with yourself. Everyone reacts to each sense differently, so if you are brilliant in another, it may have you struggling or worse, giving you nothing. Relax and go with the opening energetic flow, as your body will guide you.

So, let's explore where the psychic *sense of knowing* is located and activated.

The crown of the head is the resting place of knowing. As you may have picked up, the great activators are breath and nerve masses. The crown area is a bundle of nerves with direct brain access. Now, the brain is sensitive to infinitesimal thought patterns and can control and create entire universes. So, our thoughts are pretty basic stuff.

The mind programs, the brain computes, and the body executes; that's the process. Just as we program our computers, we program our brains to create our own personal universe.

As you think so, shall you be

You can locate this centre by placing both hands on your head. Imagine a helmet, a little like a dome, that sits just above the eyebrows. Have fun with this dome because you can, because when we have fun, we cut down on the anxiety caused by the need to *get it right*. There is no right or wrong way. There is only your way.

I like to imagine a shining silver dome, and sometimes I add many weird and wonderful attachments, so it looks like some way out-of-space thing. You can create and play with apps to give you a visual.

Having located this area, spend time sitting, hands on head, to connect and become attuned to the energy flow.

It will be interesting to keep some records. Is it stronger on some days? Does the moon cycle affect it? Is it out of control during menstrual cycles? Yes, men this applies to you and anyone living together as cycles become attuned to each other.

Sexual and touching contact blend your energies, and many become attuned to one reality on some level. It's that sense of knowing what others will think, say, and do. Finishing their sentences, knowing their moods, when they need you, and when they need to be left alone.

Knowing is a fantastic sense when activated between two energies. Yes, I said energies instead of people. In terms of the physical, this alignment can be non-sexual. It may be between mother and son, father and daughter, brother and brother, work partners, or friends. Get the picture?

Knowing each other on deep levels is an incredible gift, and often, it can be mistaken for love. It can then get muddied and confusing. Let's hold off ongoing there for now.

So, having done the locating, time to activate, yes, you got it: breathing time. Working with the centred breath technique referred to in *Housekeeping* activates and opens this psychic area.

Take a seat where you are comfortable, place your hands over the head area, and breathe. As you gently work with the centred breath, allow yourself to become aware of sensations in your body. This may start as a warmth, a tingling, or what seems like tiny electric shocks. Have no expectations and accept what comes.

If nothing, ask what kind of nothing? Nothing, as in empty? Nothing, as in no feeling? Nothing, as in *what*? Keep questioning, and you may be surprised at the answers. For, in fact, there is no actual nothing. Ask yourself, what were you expecting? Even with other things emerging, without it, you have nothing.

Dedicate a week to work with each centre for instant activation or attunement. An attunement aligns energy and awakens the connection between the human soul and energy. Having spent some time getting to know the feel of your psychic knowing, play with it. Yes, I mean play, as opposed to practice. Practice or working implies some expectation and induces stress and anxiety. Play implies freedom, fun, and the ability to experience joy and laughter.

Sit with those two attitudes, and you will *know* which pattern is the more positive. Feel free to share with your friends.

I feel the need to ask permission before playing in someone's head. Trust your physical body to guide you beyond limitations into other realms of knowledge.

Make the time to prepare. Turn off your mobile phone, use incense or music, or whatever works for you. Take your time. This is about exploring and discovering whole new realities. Relax and use the centred breathing technique for as long as you need.

As you inhale, imagine, feel, see, or *know* energy flowing from the universe to yourself. For each exhale, allow the *head area to expand* and *contract.*

Think of your head area as an antenna that returns the needed information. Allow images, thoughts, or whatever to flow into and out of your psychic centre. Be aware other centres may join in the fun because they can. So, no stress; just allow it to happen.

For example, yes, you are working on the *knowing,* but *feeling* and *gut instinct* may come along for the ride. You will learn about *gut instinct* in *Chapter Four – The Gift of Feeling.* As you become comfortable extending your energy into the universe and receiving information, you may want to move to the next level.

I find working with like-minded people stimulates and accelerates growth. Take an image or ask someone to give you a name or question. Take your time. There's no rush, nor is it a competition. It is practice, practice, practice.

You may also want to extend your *knowing* into the universe. Ask the question in your mind. What do I know of this person, place, or whatever? Breathe in the information. At this stage, try not to analyse or filter, just receive. Remember, the little odd bits may seem insignificant to you. However, they can be huge to someone else.

Years ago, a client sought a connection with her father in spirit. All I kept getting was potato fields. I tried again, and I got potatoes. I tried many times, and I got potatoes. Finally, I had to say *sorry; all I am seeing is potato fields.* She burst into tears and said her dad was a potato farmer.

You need to let go of expectations and avoid judging incoming information. The psychic sense of knowing becomes overwhelming because it is flooded with information that needs filtering. People can relate the *knowing* to the past, present, or future, adding to confusion.

Exercise - Knowing
Dedicate a few minutes each week to connect, ask, and know.

What do you want to know about the upcoming week? This can be weather, family, friends, current events, or anything. Write them down and review your answers at the end of the week and note any differences. This simple process builds confidence. Do not judge if you have an off week. Give it a month before revisiting. What knowledge did you possess before that needed time to unfold?

Remember, lighten up, relax, and have fun. Try to tune into how a situation will be before you get there. Media events offer a great opportunity to observe people's attire, much like a social gathering. If you are going for an interview, sit with it for a while and tune into the interviewer. What do you know about them? Having some insight could give you the edge.

Finish each day by acknowledging where an extra sense enhanced your experience.

Understand that this is a journey unique to you, yours alone. Enjoy it. Be the gift you came here to be.

Chapter Two – The Gift of Seeing

The *gift of seeing* is one of the most remarkable of the senses because *seeing* can be past, present, future, and so much more.

As you would have guessed by now, seeing is different for everyone, so stick with what works for you. If a process adds to your experience, fantastic. The more we learn, the more we know, the more we share, the more the universe unites.

Let's begin by exploring, locating, and activating.

The location is at the back of the eyes and upwards. In fact, our eyes hold activated silver chakra centres, and once activated, there is no turning back.

Place one hand over your eyes and the other at the base of your skull. You may feel a shimmering vibration. Having connected on this level, look up, rolling your eyes as far back in your head as possible. This will initially feel strange and may be uncomfortable as it is another unused set of muscles getting a workout.

Continue practising, as there is a lot to be gained here. Once you can do this without stress, the next bit is easy and is like child's play.

Close your eyes and look up. Yes, that's it. The process is done and dusted.

However, I will introduce you to some processes that enhance the experience as you move through your journey.

To see

To *see* has many forms and dimensions. You may see a video playing in your head, images that float through, movie scenes, scenes from your life, or words. The connections are endless. However, they may or may not be accurate or precise.

This is a tricky sense, and it often plays games with our minds. You may see a friend and wonder, what's that about? It could be the person you read for may have a friend with the same name, or perhaps experience holds the answer, or you should consult that friend.

Seeing is the most frustrating of all the senses because it may be fleeting and past, present, and future rolled into one. Also, it is hard not to blurt out what you see. I've learned that not everyone wants to know or believe what you *see*. Discretion is a tough learning curve.

I get what I call snapshots, little postage stamp size images that float in and out quickly, a bit like you *catch me if you can*.

When we use the psychic sense of seeing, we open a huge doorway to other dimensions and realities. I never question things I see now. Experience has taught me there's always a reason.

One of my favourite things is to sit in a park and watch people pass by. Seeing various things around people, like colours, children, animals and places, is enjoyable. Unlike others, I don't run up to strangers to deliver messages.

If someone comes to me for guidance, fine. If not, for me, it is crossing a personal boundary. We need absolute ethics when opening our psychic centres. We will never be the same when they are open and ready to go. And so, each of us needs to develop our own personal ethics.

Higher sight

Higher sight is an amazing sense that expands and grows, sometimes in its own way. There are ways to reach higher levels, such as *past life*, *remote viewing* and *projection* into other realms.

Not everyone can reach these levels, as they are not for everyone. It can be a choice. Not everyone wants to go to university and is happy with their education. The gift of *seeing* is similar.

We will take the next step now, and you can see where it takes you and choose your personal direction.

Connecting with the universal mind happens effortlessly, often subconsciously. Once you've focused on the area around your eyes, *look up,* as mentioned before. Yes, that is it—easy as.

You will become aware that the head area needs to expand as you focus. Keep flicking those eyes *up*. You are now in a space to receive information. So, having located and activated, let's play with it.

Think of a friend or family member and see what is happening around them. You can confirm what happens later. Try sending them a simple message, a call, or a repeated word.

I find it most rewarding to play this *game* with friends. So, have someone agree to share the experience with you. Send them a thought and have them call you back and confirm. Then have them send you a thought. These thoughts may come as images. Or you may like to have them pick up something, focus on it, and vary the game to allow your sense to grow.

This is a precursor to *remote viewing,* which is not covered in this book for ethical reasons.

If you desire, tune in for a quick glimpse of your day and ask for directions. Not being a shopper, I check out what I want beforehand. I usually go straight to it with no problems. I admit to being an *op shop* addict and know when I must go to a particular shop, my favourite being The Salvation Army. Sometimes, I must search for what I need, making the husband run away, and indeed, it is there.

As with everything, you need to practice, practice, and do more practice. You also need to validate and keep validating, as this creates confidence.

Sunrise and sunset

Sunrise and sunset are two of the most significant times to restore and re-activate the vision centres, both physical and psychic.

As we are aware, it is foolhardy to gaze at the sun. Looking at the sun as she wakes up at sunrise is okay. It is *not okay* to look at the sun at any other time of the day, as it is too strong.

However, just as the sun wakes up and retires for the night, there are moments of pure magic. It is a time when it is possible to walk between the worlds.

Sit in an outside space that brings you peace. This can be the beach, a park, or your own backyard. The place is not important, but the act of sitting in an outside space is.

Process

Face the rising or setting sun.

Close your eyes and relax. Take long, slow breaths.

Notice what you *see:* lights, shapes, or anything.

Gently observe, push nothing, hold no expectations, just be in the moment.

After a few minutes, open your eyes and briefly gaze at the sun.

Notice what you see and what you feel.

This simple act can re-vitalise you for the day ahead or relax you after a hectic day.

Extended vision

We only use a fraction of our sight, and we *see* from the centre of the eye only—our point of focus. However, there is definitely more to *see*.

Have you *seen* something out of the corner of your eye? A flash of light or a figure that disappears when you attempt to focus on it? These are seen with extended vision, using the whole eye. Now, this is not easy to change.

The following process, done regularly, will extend your physical and psychic vision range.

Process

Sit down and get comfortable. Relax your eyes for a few minutes. It's as simple as closing your eyes.

Open your eyes. Look to the right as far as possible without moving your head. Hold to the count of five, then return to the centre.

Look to the left as far as possible without moving your head. Hold to the count of five, then come back to the centre.

Look up as far as possible without moving your head. Hold to the count of five, then come back to the centre.

Look down as far as possible without moving your head. Hold to the count of five, then come back to the centre.

Now, looking straight ahead, *see* if the range of vision has grown.

Repeat this process at least three times. Each time, note how much further you can see.

By training our eyes, we expand our vision and line of sight.

Vision versus seeing

Is there a difference between *vision* and *seeing*? I would have to say absolutely. To *see*, we use our physical eyes, and the focus is outward. Vision is the *inner eye* wanting to focus and connect, allowing an understanding of things not yet formed in the physical world.

When someone is born blind or loses sight, they naturally become more focused on the inner self. Other senses are heightened and take over.

So, it is between vision and seeing. When we close our eyes, our inner vision switches on. This is a natural progression. We don't need to do anything.

You should understand these natural psychic abilities, so let's not interfere. Just tune in to your own rhythms.

Meditate with your eyes closed, then focus on your breath and let your vision do its thing.

Mind you, vision is not always a person's strong point. Some do not *see*. They feel or know, although this is all still an inner vision.

When we close our eyes, we open the doors for another awareness to emerge. The distractions of *seeing* are closed out, and we can centre and focus.

Now it's time to do some exercises. The following exercises are about having fun. It will become a chore and not a learning game if you are too serious. So, have fun.

Group exercise – Seeing

To recap seeing, try this exercise a few times. It will become a fun activity with friends and a lesson in awareness.

As the leader, for the session choose one colour in a crowded area: at the shop, in the park, at the beach, or anywhere you choose.

Choose two colours per session but avoid choosing more than two until you gain experience.

Set a time for 10 minutes using a timer or your mobile phone timer. Tell everyone the colour and encourage them to focus on seeing that one colour as much as possible. After 10 minutes, everyone except you should compare their observations.

Close your eyes and let the images appear. How much more do you see? How much clearer is the detail? Do you now notice insignificant details, like the writing on a coffee cup?

What this exercise accomplishes is two-fold. It brings about activated vision and recall and extends the awareness of your surroundings.

Single person exercise – Seeing

As you travel on a bus or train, consciously *see* the other passengers. When you arrive home, sit quietly, close your eyes, and recall what you can *see*. Do you *see* what you missed with open eyes?

Chapter Three – The Gift of Hearing

The *gift of hearing*, in the hearing centre, is strong in many people, and more so now than ever. As the vibrational energies shift, we notice that attunements are in progress.

Do you have any thoughts on the buzzing that comes and goes? Some experience this as extending out from inside the ear, while others experience it coming into the ear. Both are fine. It is just another way of receiving. Again, take baby steps to locate and activate.

The physical space extends behind the head above the ears. As noted, these areas are full of nerve endings that speak directly to the brain, which extends into the universal consciousness. Hence, we have access to all that is.

Historically, people severed ears from gypsies and fortune tellers, telling us a thing or two about their fear. There was also an awareness of the power of hearing. People believed gypsies could extend their hearing abilities, enabling them to spy and gain secrets. Incidentally, it's closer to the truth than you realise.

Let me share with you a practice I learned many, many years ago. It is called *eating the sun*, which aims to extend our hearing range and beyond.

Eating the sun

The sun is an amazing energy source that gives us a daily shot of Vitamin D and tunes us into universal energy on very deep levels. This simple shamanic practice does so much to align your spirit and heal your soul.

The first few times you practice this process are about the activation of the hearing sense.

Each morning just after sunrise:

Sit quietly, facing the sun. Take some slow, gentle breaths and close your eyes. Allow the colours and patterns to emerge. Relax for around five minutes.

Place your thumbs behind each ear, then bring your fingers to join at the back of your head low down, encasing the lower bony ridge. Then, carry on with the exercise.

After a few tries, you will find this sense naturally clicks in whenever you focus on extending hearing.

Turn your head left, so the sun falls on your head behind your ear. As the sun's heat warms your head, expand your sense of hearing.

Turn your head right so the sun falls on your head behind your ear. Expand your sense of hearing as the sun's heat warms your head.

Lower your head towards your chest, allowing the sun to warm the top of your head.

Shut your eyes and look towards the sun again. Move your eyes in an arch: left, up, right, repeat a few times. Gently open your eyes.

Note how things appear for the next few minutes. You may experience a heightened sense of vision. You may see the life force of plants.

Remember, this is solely your experience, so enjoy.

The more you practice, the more you will hear. Before starting, I check how far away I can hear and afterwards, while rechecking, it is always much further. I've managed to get it three blocks away. Also, this allows messages to *be heard*. What is the natural world telling you?

The more practised you become, the more attuned you are to hear more and understand the language of *your* soul. It is different for everyone, so do not judge your experience by that of others. Some get a lot quickly, and others need patience in opening up to *hearing*.

I hear the messages from the crows, but I have always had an affinity with them. My family has always called me *Crow*. I hear the changes in the wind that carry emotions. Now, some of us do the *oh my gosh, I am going mad, I am hearing things*, or *I am talking to myself*. Yes, some of us, maybe. However, most of us tune in to the psychic hearing centre.

I find I *hear* in my voice, which I know can be confusing. However, I do not hear words or expressions I would use in normal conversation or sounds that are not around me.

For instance, I did a reading for one client, and all I heard throughout the reading were trains. Now, we were in a coastal country area with no trains. There were never any trains. The client was as confused as me. Later, she rang to let me know she had discovered her grandfather had, in fact, been involved in designing and building railways. So be aware everything means something to someone.

In another reading for a different client, I did a recording and it had nothing but frogs chatting away. There were no frogs in town, especially in 40-degree-plus heat. I had to wonder why I was there, and I will tell you the story.

Two years later, the lady returned to Australia with an intriguing story. After the reading, she went to England on a working holiday with her fiancé. On New Year's Eve, the reading made sense. I had seen her in a castle, with her true love by her side. They had booked into this amazing, gracious old mansion—a castle.

The evening started wonderfully, and they were served the most delicious dinner in the main hall. When they went to the ballroom in the evening, the fiancé disappeared briefly. She used the extended sense of hearing I had taught her to find him. It's a big request in such a vast space. She saw him in the arms of another woman, whispering sweet nothings and planning to meet up later.

As in all the good stories, she confronted them and ran, not knowing where she was heading. She ended up at a lake, where the frogs were singing. She said there were hundreds of them.

Wait for it. Having left the party for a smoke, a young man selflessly shared his coat and more with her. To the best of my knowledge, they returned together to Australia and lived happily ever after.

✦ ✦ ✦

How does one work with psychic hearing? It is easy. You should understand as all this is as natural as breathing. It will naturally do its thing, and we must be aware of it. It is admittedly unethical and rude to listen to others' conversations, but it offers valuable practice. I do not mean tuning in to pick up the latest gossip; I mean receiving relevant information and feedback.

Is going out, partying, projecting, and listening lively, boring, or helpful? If it's boring, then plan your escape. If you are thinking of joining a group, what do you hear around it? Is it progressive? Is it good for you? Ask the questions. When going out to dinner, check the restaurant and listen. It could mean the difference between a great night and a disaster.

The more we work with the physical sense of hearing, the more alert the psychic sense becomes. While working alongside others, you may come across the strangest occurrences, as I have mentioned before. Examples are particular music, television shows, names of people and places, statements, and messages are all part of the process.

I sometimes hear accidents, the whole thing, then I know if it is past or about to happen. If it is in the future, I wait for backup information, which often comes with a blend of the psychic senses.

Because no sense works independently, they all fuse and blend, some stronger than others at different times. After all, the physical senses complete the job, simultaneously walking, talking, and listening. Humans really are a wondrous creation.

For me, the wind is linked to the sense of hearing, so I will share a bit of its magic with you.

The wind

There is a song I love by John Denver, *Windsong*[1], which has these lyrics:

The wind is the whisper of our mother the earth.
The wind is the hand of our father the sky.
The wind watches over our struggles and pleasures.
The wind is the goddess who first learned to fly.
The wind is the bearer of bad and good tidings, the weaver of darkness, the bringer of dawn.
The wind gives the rain, then builds us a rainbow, the wind is the singer who sang the first song.
The wind is a twister of anger and warming, the wind brings the fragrance of freshly mown hay.
The wind is a racer, a wild stallion running and the sweet taste of love on a slow summer's day.

---

[1] https://johndenver.com/albums/windsong/.

The wind knows the songs of cities and canyons, the thunder of mountains, the roar of the sea.
The wind is the taker and giver of mornings, the wind is the symbol of all that is free.
So welcome the wind and the wisdom she offers, follow her summons when she calls again.
In your heart and your spirit, let the breezes surround you.
Lift up your voice then and sing with the wind.

Working with the wind

The wind has incredible energies to cleanse and renew if we allow it. Those stormy, windy days clear the old, making way for the new. When that happens, open all doors and windows and allow the wind to circulate and carry all the stale energies from your home. You could also walk on the beach in the wind or stand in high places and allow the wind to blow through your hair.

Archangels and the wind

Archangels complement the energies of the winds beautifully, while adding an enormous boost of energy, protection and love to everything we connect with.

You can work with the Archangels and the wind to provide some protection. In working with the Archangels, it is important to review and modify the process each time.

East: When the wind blows from the east, call on the energies of Archangel Raphael to blow away mental issues and illness, and to soothe anxiety and release fears.

South: When the wind blows from the south, call on the energies of Archangel Michael to blow away anger, clear aggressive situations, and release past relationships to allow space for the new.

West: When the wind blows from the west, call on Archangel Gabriel to blow away emotional issues to release, and renew to take away guilt and jealousy, and heal emotional rifts.

North: When the north wind blows, call on Archangel Uriel to release the past and bring new beginnings. This is to let go of the troubles that weigh us down, and to release burdens and bury that which we no longer need. You don't need an elaborate rite or ceremony.

What all this means is to face the wind with your arms outspread. Allow the elements to do their thing.

According to mythology, there are four Greek gods of the wind. *Boreas* is the god of the north wind and of winter. It blows away sadness and opens up a space for new beginning.

I've always connected deeply to the south wind and love to chat. *Notus*, the Greek god of the south wind and of the summer brings joy and excitement into our reality.

Eurus, the god of the east wind ushers in the gentle winds of autumn. It gifts us peace and understanding and allows us to be free from anger and grief.

Zephyrus, the god of the west wind, relates to spring and bringing forth new ideas, allowing the old to be blown away. It opens our hearts to the natural world.

You would be wise to listen to the wisdom of the wind, for it carries so much information.

A really great exercise is to sit in silence. Listen to the land. Listen to the wind. Listen to your soul.

Calling the Archangels

I like to work with the Archangels and use the method set out below as my go-to process, whether I'm out or settling in for the night. It's uncomplicated yet effective.

Process

Sit quietly and close your eyes. Clearly see in your mind what requires protection. Say out loud or in your mind the following:

Before me Archangel Raphael
Detect, reflect, protect
On my right hand, Archangel Micheal
Detect, reflect, protect
Behind me Archangel Gabriel
Detect, reflect, protect
On my left hand, Archangel Uriel
Detect, reflect, protect.

Ways to boost your psychic senses

There are many ways to add a little enthusiasm to our psychic abilities. The following are just a few to act as stepping stones along your path to boost your psychic senses.

1. Listen

Developing your psychic abilities so you can clearly hear the guidance from spirit and sounds improves your listening and ability!

Listening to the surrounding sounds is a great way to quiet your thoughts. Listen to others when they are talking instead of thinking about what you will say next. Listen to your breath flowing in and out when you are meditating. Listen to the surrounding sounds when you sleep at night or when outside. Listen so you can clearly hear!

Quiet the voice of your ego mind to become aware of all the surrounding sounds. When you quiet your mind and listen, you will naturally be more receptive to hearing the guidance of spirit.

2. Imagine

A great way to understand how your psychic abilities works is to imagine hearing something!

This simple exercise is a workout to develop your psychic abilities, making it easier to hear spirit in the future. To do this, find a quiet spot, sit down, and imagine the sounds around you. Imagine hearing rain falling, birds chirping, a piano playing, a car horn honking, laughter, ocean waves and a dog barking. Feel free to add to this list.

Practice imagining sounds until you can clearly hear them in your mind. Notice how your inner voice sounds and where these sounds are located in your mind.

3. Meditate

You knew this one was coming, right?

Meditation is essential in developing psychic abilities and all of your subtle psychic senses. When your mind is clear and calm, you are in a state of allowing spiritual guidance to appear.

It is the most natural of all the psychic energy fields, one most of us use daily.

4. Stillness

When we are still, we are more able to become aware of our inner worlds. To become attuned to the rhythms of our physical bodies and so learn to trust in ourselves.

The heart

The heart area deserves some special time alone, for it is an individual that relates to the whole. Science has proven that the heart has a nervous system and functions independently. The heart, a centre of unity, is the soul's home.

We are taught that a heart chakra aligns with a chakra system which lives along our spinal area, outside the physical body. However, we also have a higher heart chakra near the breastbone joint as described in *Chapter Six – Chakra System*. The colour is turquoise, and it swirls rather than spins. I have seen some amazing patterns created within this area.

Also, when major surgery or injury has occurred in this area, the only essence that will heal it is *love*, whether loving attention or vibrational.

The big mamma of them all is *the sacred heart chakra*. Yes, everyone has a *sacred heart chakra*. The colours are red and gold.

Gypsy Maggie Rose

Some will remember the images of Jesus and Mary from our youth, where the heart sits outside the body. Well, guess what? The sacred heart sits beyond your body at the edge of your auric body and is the centre from which we send and receive *love*.

Chapter Four – The Gift of Feeling

The *gift of feeling* is an incredible sense and can be present, at times, as being vulnerable. The *psychic* feeling is the most natural and arguably the easiest sense of all the psychic energy fields to open and interpret. It is the one most of us use daily.

It is the best *psychic* sense for discerning and interpreting subtle energies, empathising with others and for personal protection.

How many times have you heard the phrase *gut instinct*? If you have, then welcome to the energy of feeling. You may recall reading about this in

Chapter One – The Gift of Knowing. Yes, that's right but you are now learning about the *gift of feeling.*

Most of us have had times when we have *listened* to our *gut feeling* or *gut instinct* and have seen amazing results. I know the few times I have had my gut screaming to run and ignored it. While expected, the results were not welcome.

I believe that this is our first instinct and that we are connected via the umbilical cord to the responses of our mother. We *learn* so much in the womb that affects the rest of our lives. I understand there is scientific proof that we were carried in our grandmother's womb when she carried us. Our mother carried all her eggs before birth, so we are generational beings; we carry the memories and pass them forward.

What we need to understand is that everyone and everything has a vibrational pattern, and tuning into these patterns allows us to access the *psychic* world around us. If one person has achieved something, it is achievable by anyone, regardless of who they are.

Like the physical, the psychic senses also interpret and react to stimuli. Just as we learn to walk, talk and listen, we can see how great we are at learning to use natural assets. Harnessing psychic energies is easy, with a touch of gypsy magic as the final touch.

In reality, the entire human body is a highly efficient antenna. It can tune into and interpret inner energies, allowing the vibrations to work in absolute balance with the universe. All we need to do is get out of its way and get on with living life as we were designed to.

When working with clients, I usually feel physical issues from their late family and friends. The first thing I feel is often the last thing they feel, like chest pain or being shot—the feelings are intense. I also feel their emotions and love and, unfortunately, sometimes anger and frustration. I can't handle violent issues, and it sometimes results in unexpected vomiting. On air or during a presentation, it's not a good look, but it's expected when working with many clients.

Remember, this *psychic feeling* is tuned specifically to you, so your experience might differ.

What are the hallmarks of a person high in feeling?
A person with heightened *psychic* sensitivity deeply cares for the well-being of all living beings, whether they have fur, feathers, fins, flesh, or flora. Usually, you can sense when someone is troubled. You trust your gut feelings. There is no genuine concern around timelines or deadlines; you sort of drift in and out of time and space. You try to put people at ease and expect others to have the same caring attitude.

A person strong in psychic feeling is highly sensitive to the emotions of others and gives sincerely, making them the ultimate *people* person. They trust their feelings, are flexible and adaptable to others, and are the best touchy-huggy type.

A person high in feeling needs to be aware they are prone to pick up the feelings of others—the good, the bad and the ugly. They can become psychically overloaded and overwhelmed, may have trouble with times and deadlines, and are susceptible to being hurt by rejection.

How does it feel?
A person high in *psychic* feeling needs to protect themselves against the emotions of others. Sometimes, it can feel like an emotional deluge. They experience a feeling where they get overwhelmed by the emotions of others, which can feel like an invasion, but they do not know of its source. I find shopping centres a nightmare. Do you?

When you can understand that some of the negative feelings may, in fact, not be yours, it is a starting point.

Some examples are tension, anxiety, anger and depression, which are heavier energies, and as such, they hang around longer.

Identifying where an emotion fits in the overall picture allows you to take action and quickly release it. A person high in psychic feelings needs to regularly clear their energy fields.

Where is the feeling centre located?

The psychic feeling centre is the one centre most linked to physical sensations. You may experience it as a slight flutter in your heart, a knot in your belly, or you have a need to, and do, throw up.

This centre covers the autonomic involuntary nervous system, in the stomach region and provides a direct pathway to the subconscious mind for psychic impressions and feelings.

This is the big one, as the involuntary nervous system links to every major organ and most glands in the body, including direct communication to the brain. Its purpose is to regulate the body's automatic functions, including blood pressure and pulse.

In fact, you name it, this has it covered. It lies from just beneath the breastbone to just below the navel. It begins at the belly button and radiates towards the throat and pelvic regions.

Physically, this is where most things happen. No wonder we react and feel so many emotions in this area.

There is a lot of research in the medical field that supports the gut–brain connection with many states of dis-ease traceable to it. I was most surprised to hear that the latest research connects diseases such as *Parkinson's* to the gut-brain connection. It appears to be formed in the gut and travels to the brain via the Vagus nerve, the superhighway.

Interestingly, the Vagus nerve is connected to most of the internal organs.

We can check our health by tuning into this nerve as our *gut feelings* travel along this superhighway to the brain. We shouldn't be surprised that science shows what our ancestors instinctively knew.

The Vagus nerve also takes in a few chakra centres, significantly the *solar plexus*, where the *physical* meets the *spiritual*. This area takes us beyond the physical into the realms of so much, including past lives, survival, and creativity. I provide a summary of the chakra centres in *Chapter Six – Chakra System*.

Once we have located the involuntary nervous system in the stomach region, we can start the activation process. Although it may be functioning well, there's still room for improvement.

How to activate the feeling centre

Belly breathing activates this centre, giving everything a massive kick start. The key to activating the feeling centre is *belly breathing*. If you have not tried the precursor, *belly breath*, go back to *Housekeeping* and go for it.

Belly breathing

Belly breathing is an extension of the *belly breath* process set out in *Housekeeping*. It is connected to, and works with, the feeling centre. *This section is about working with belly breathing.* The key is to try—if you haven't, go back and give it a shot.

Another way I *tune* into this centre is using a crystal, which is fine if you are home or in bed. It is easy to sit or lay with a crystal in your belly button, but what about when you are out and about? Most people wear a ring, at least one with a crystal. Remember, a diamond is a crystal. Turn the ring inwards and place your hand over the belly button. How easy is that?

Sometimes, the hearing centre takes on a life of its own—it's the protection thing. Personally, I find this psychic sense unstable in crowds and shopping centres. Remember to ensure you have protection in place before entering such spaces. If unable to do so, enclose yourself with a light cage or shield all sides of yourself [these protections are not covered in this book].

Exercise – Feeling

Walk around your street, a park, the beach, or wherever you fancy. With the ring mentioned above, turn the ring around and activate the centre. As you walk, become aware of any subtle feelings from houses, people, animals, or whatever.

Lower the centre, remove your hand, and see if you feel a change. If you get bad feelings from somewhere or someone, put your protection in place and have feel again.

Quite fascinating, really. I often get weird feelings while travelling in places or cars around me. When you realise an aura extends beyond a car, it is possible to pick up feelings from the inhabitants. It's challenging to put away your aura, like rolling up an airbag, but that won't happen.

So, get out there and practice. Feelings can be picked up as emotions, so it may be wise to question where some of your feelings are coming from. Be still and focus. Is this emotion yours? If so, why are you feeling it? If not, where did it come from, and what actions can you take? Using music to work with psychic centres is great.

Hearing: What do you hear, the melody, the words? What do they mean to you? Who do they bring to mind? Do they invoke a memory?

Seeing: This can be tougher. What images does the music invoke? Are they memories or dreams?

Knowing: What do you just know? What is the music evoking? What is the music or lyrics saying to you? How do you know the message?

Feeling: Wow, this tends to be the big one for me. How does the music feel to you? What is the music drawing up emotionally? How do you respond to music? Do you dance? Do you cry?

Working with music allows energy to flow more freely. Often, what we cannot express in words, we can express release through music.

There have been many times I have sobbed through a state of distress, accompanied by music, mainly John Denver. I loved that man. I've also danced in a frenzy during rituals and partied my heart out in celebration.

Oh, what a sad, sad world we would be without music. Do you think you can even imagine watching a movie without music? Music builds our excitement and response. So, make music a part of the creative process of living.

How can feeling help you?

So how can *feeling* help you? It acts as an alarm, alerting you to take care. If you go to unfamiliar places, sit quietly, and have a *feel* ahead of time. What is your gut telling you? How does it feel? Are you excited, scared, nervous, good, bad?

Then, check how the feeling feels. Does it feel bad for you? In a dangerous way or as a negative experience? Ask questions about the feelings you get. Explore, evaluate, and gain confidence in your decisions by questioning who, how, why, what, and where.

Feeling can be of amazing use in making important life choices, like where to live, or whether this car is safe.

Added extra belly button joy

We ignore one of the most important points of the physical body—the good old belly button. Through this area, we receive nourishment and develop in the womb, forming our first connections to our mother. This area is a rich centre where all nerve endings meet and travel throughout the body and beyond. Yet, it is an unknown or ignored area.

Ancient wisdom taught us the importance of a divine connection with *omphalos*, the belly button.

From the stump of the umbilical cord, nerves extend to the entire body. As such, we can use them to heal quickly and to connect with our deeper selves. How many of us pay attention to this area when we are unwell? I mean unwell anywhere in the body, physical, mental, or emotionally. I can assure there are not many people who do.

So, let's get back in connection with the Vagus nerve superhighway. It's straightforward, and we all have the ability to accomplish it.

Your body does not lie

This is about how to tune into the truth of your body. In reality, your body cannot and will not lie to you. This simple process helps clear the confusion and uncertainty. The following exercise may help you understand how your body behaves under certain circumstances.

Pain control

Dealing with pain is a daily struggle for most of us. To explore the function of the Vagus nerve as a brain pathway, consider trying the exercise below. There are, however, practices available to assist and, in many cases, relieve the associated stress. The balance shifts when we take control and decide to *do something* about it.

Standing up to the pain is often a way to regain control. I have seen the process below work many times and have used it with significant effect. It always amazes me how we forget to help ourselves, using our knowledge but offering others the needed wisdom and assistance. Allow *self-care*.

Exercise – Feeling (in pain control)

The breathing described here has healing and centreing advantages.

First, begin by concentrating on your breath. Breathe deeply, but only to the point before it becomes discomfort.

Breathe in until just before it becomes uncomfortable. Breathe out just before it becomes uncomfortable. Repeat until you feel relaxed and calm.

Bring to mind the site of your pain. Where is it situated? Then, breathe into that pain. Breathing with the pain gives you some control. Breathe in as the pain builds. Breathe out as it subsides.

Now begins the magic.

Picture the pain in your mind. Make it real; give it an identity. *What shape is it?* Is it round, square, flat, jagged? What is the shape? Breathe until you can clearly see, feel, or know the shape. *What colour is it?* Is it red, blue, green, what colour? When you see, feel or know the colour, what shade is it? Is it clear, murky, vibrant, shadowy?

Breathe into it. *What does it smell like?* Allow the taste of the pain to surface. Is it sweet, metallic, nasty?

Breathe into it. *What does it taste like?* Allow yourself to identify the taste of the pain. Is it sweet, sour, metallic, vile, or bloody?

Breathe into it. *What does it feel like?* Is it soft, squishy, hard, bouncy, strong, weak, prickly?

Breathe into it. *Now, give it a name.* Having given the pain a clear identity. *How can you destroy it?* Can it be smashed, run over, shattered, belted, bombed, frozen, or melted? The clearer the image, the better. In your mind, pick up a weapon to destroy the pain. Whatever it takes, a hammer, a cannon, a bomb, a dragon, an iceberg. The choice is yours. Then, in your mind, destroy the pain.

Exercise – Feeling

Walk around your street, a park, the beach, or wherever you fancy. Turn the ring around and activate the centre. As you walk, become aware of any subtle feelings from houses, people, animals, or whatever.

Lower the centre, remove your hand, and see if you feel a change. Got yukky feelings from somewhere or someone. Put your protection in place and have another feel.

Quite fascinating, really. I often get weird feelings while travelling in places or cars around me. When you realise an aura extends beyond the car, it is possible to pick up feelings from the inhabitants. It's challenging to put away your aura, like rolling up an airbag, but that won't happen.

So, get out there and practice. Feelings can be picked up as emotions, so it may be wise to question where some of your feelings are coming from. Be still and focus. Is this emotion yours? If so, why are you feeling it? If not, where did it come from, and what actions can you take? Using music to work with psychic centres is great.

Gypsy Maggie Rose

Hearing: What do you hear, the melody, the words? What do they mean to you? Who do they bring to mind? Do they invoke a memory?

Seeing: This can be tougher. What images does the music invoke? Are they memories or dreams?

Knowing: What do you just know? What is the music evoking? What is the music or lyrics saying to you? How do you know the message?

Feeling: Wow, this tends to be the big one for me. How does the music feel to you? What is the music drawing up emotionally? How do you respond to music? Dance? Cry?

Working with music allows energy to flow more freely. Often, what we cannot express in words, we can express release through music.

There have been many times I have sobbed through a state of distress, accompanied by music, mainly John Denver. I loved that man. I've also danced in a frenzy during rituals and partied my heart out in celebration.

Oh, what a sad, sad world we would be without music. Do you think you can even imagine watching a movie without music? That builds our excitement and response. So, make music part of the creative process of living.

Exercise – Feeling

Give yourself space to adapt to this activation, which is likely already active within most of us.

When you do not focus on getting it right, you achieve better results because the process becomes simpler.

Place both hands over the belly button and breathe. Yes, just breathe. Play music, put a crystal on your belly button, or anything else—the choice is yours. The experience needs to be tuned to you.

On the out breath, expand your reality. Reach out through this area. Visualise a person, breathe, and notice the accompanying emotions.

Some people find they want to share their experiences. If that is you, practising with people who work in the media is great because there is feedback. You can also work with a partner or friend.

After you have finished, make a note of what you feel. The more you practice, the more confident you will become. There will come a time, often quickly, when you *do it* as a regular part of living.

Exercise – Feeling

Relax and take some time to *centre your breath*. Take some long, slow breaths just before it becomes uncomfortable. Gently let the breath out to where it is uncomfortable. Repeat until it feels like a natural rhythm.

In your mind, ask yourself a totally honest question. Your answer has to be the absolute truth. The question can be as simple as your name and address. Keep asking the same question over and over for two minutes.

Now, *feel* how your body responds. You are sensing for a feeling, not words or images, a feeling. How does it *feel? G*o deep in that thought. Go with that feeling and let yourself go deep within it.

Now, tell yourself an absolute lie. Make sure it is an outrageous lie. How does it *feel?* Go deep with the feeling. This is your gauge. Can you feel the difference? If you use it often, it will become second nature.

Learn to tune into yourself. Ask yourself what you are feeling. Do not accept *nothing* as an answer. If nothing, what kind of nothing? Is nothing different? Is nothing a void? Nothing, as in something, is missing? Keep asking and feeling until you understand what you are feeling.

Also, ask yourself if you are feeling good or bad and why you feel that way. Consider where these feelings come from and if they are fleeting or permanent. Following a path and continuing the questioning, we enter a relaxed state, where the subconscious allows images and answers to float up.

Sensing spirit

In the *feeling centre*, sensing spirit is something you may have felt or encountered but have not been able to put a name to it or known how to deal with it.

As I have connected with the psychic centres and moved into the realms of connecting with spirit, I have compiled some things you may encounter.

I love a good ghost hunt, but it takes some sorting out when we begin or try to bring it all together.

Here are some things you may encounter or already be familiar with.

In preparing to sense spirt activity and presence, vigorously rub your hands together. This notifies your senses, that *hey we are going in guys, get ready for action*. Then centre your breath and go for it.

Cold spots

Often, cold spots can indicate the presence of a spirit form. Either the room becomes cold, or a spot in one area of the room will suddenly become cold. Make sure to walk slowly around the space and feel with your hands, or you might *step* into a cold area. This may be as simple as a few degrees colder or freezing. It can also be a cold breeze on a hot summer day.

Hot spots

Exactly the same for cold spots, which can vary from warm to intense. Or you may become intensely cold or hot. Hot spots tend to be smaller in area and confined to one space. For instance, you may sense the pre-existence of a fireplace in an abandoned ruin. You may also feel heat where disturbing or violent events took place.

Rapping, scratching, knocking
One way spirit can communicate is through sound. Often, strange knockings indicate that a spirit form is close at hand. Objects can also be dropped, moved, or thrown. Objects thrown are usually poltergeist activity. Chain dragging might be true in old castles, but I've never heard it despite visiting a few. Mind you, I have occasionally heard my name called clearly and loudly. Once, an abusive voice suggested that I *shut the f**king door*.

Energy drains and equipment malfunctions
When a spirit draws energy to become visible, it often draws on nearby energy. This energy can come from batteries in video cameras and other devices. When spirit is present, cameras, tape recorders, and even lights are suddenly unstable or stop working.

I have had equipment blow up, never to be used again. Interestingly, power often returns to the equipment once you leave the area where it is located.

Often, one of the first contacts a departed friend or family member makes is via turning lights on and off, although sometimes it is something else. The gas was always shut off in the house where my mother once lived. She couldn't cook because the gas burners and oven were always off when she returned from going out. This is not great for baking a cake. Needless to say, she never stayed there for long.

Physical sensations

Physical encounters can occur, such as the sensation of being touched, pinched, or slapped. This includes the instant knowledge of injuries or the cause of passing. Often, a soft breeze at the back of the neck. A feeling of walking into something solid.

Smells

These smells can seem to come from nowhere and develop and disappear just as quickly. The smells can vary from sweet floral scents and tobacco to putrid smells. Smells can often give clues to the habits of the spirit entity. It can also indicate the presence of *angels*.

Tastes

It is possible to receive a taste sensation and know what you are tasting. Tastes also indicate the habits of the spirit entity. Sometimes, during a reading, I taste alcohol that was liked by the one who departed. In dealing with cancer, I always experience a weird taste that I call chemo, which it probably isn't in the real world. But it is my indicator during readings, and you may find similar things turn up for you.

Mists and other masses
You may see spirit manifestations as strange shadows and black masses. They might also appear as wispy forms, like smoke or fleeting, foggy, incomplete images, or as a patch of fog on a summer day.

Apparitions
Occasionally, some spirits may appear as barely visible forms or may be as solid and normal looking like a living person. Spirits can reveal their past lives through your eyes. Often, I see people walking through the house when I know no one is there. I've had moments when I thought I saw someone, and they appeared later in the day. Work with your senses to align things your way.

Disembodied voices
These sounds can be whispers, moans, or even shouts, and yes, they can be scary. I have often heard my name called, and no one was there. I sometimes answer the door, but no one is there despite hearing the doorbell. My phone often rings, and nothing or the blessed thing dials someone, and I am like, *what the heck*.

Orbs and light anomalies
Spirit energy can occasionally appear as orbs of light or anomalies, such as flickering forms. Orbs vary in size and colour and are visible to the naked eye and on camera. You should also be aware that *some* orbs caught on camera are water or dust particles. However, they are very easy to distinguish. Also, shadow, smoky

film, and other images can and do appear in photos. After taking the photo, some images of people develop years later. Today's technology allows cameras to capture significantly more. Also, the veils between the worlds are much thinner, making the task more manageable.

Aura

All of us have extended *energy,* the most familiar being the *aura.* So, let's examine what we know about it. Everything and everyone has an aura. It is an electromagnetic field reflecting everything that occurs within the physical, mental, and emotional structures. Some people see auras as colour reflected around the person. Others *know* and *feel* the boundaries and the vibration. Each is equally correct, as there is no one-size-fits-all. The aura reflects the inner body language, allowing for another dimension of insight.

Objects, even non-living ones, like furniture and pictures, possess an aura. The aura can sometimes be difficult to view, but it pops up for some. You cannot see an aura by staring at an object or person. You should use soft eyes, allowing the eyes to become slightly out of focus. Look through the eyelashes or look just beyond the object or person.

Say you need to check out a person, then relax, let your eyes become soft and focus just behind their shoulders. It is easier if you have either a black or white background. There is a need to be aware of a false aura reading.

Becoming acquainted with the colour wheel is essential. Learn which colours are complementary, as these can affect the vision. Staring at a colour for any time can cause a bleached effect.

Say if you are focusing on a person and they are wearing a bright yellow shirt or dress. Then, if you slightly shift your eyes or look at a white wall, you will probably see purple, blue or violet. Seeing red around yellow shows an actual aura colour. So, make the colour wheel your friend. If the colours are not complementary, they are most likely auric and is a false aura reading.

People watching

People watching is a great way to sense aura. Choose a park or mall with a bustling atmosphere to sit among people. Shift your attention upwards and gently focus your attention on a person or animal. Do not stare or force anything—gently, gently. Look a little beyond them or above their heads. Typically, the initial sight is a slightly lighter band. Trees are amazing for aura practice with early morning and evening the best. Gently focus on one side as an aura is often seen as bands of light around them.

Remember, the more you relax, the more you see, feel, and know. Also, remember that this needs to be how you do it.

Auras have two dimensions: shape and colour. It is equally important to note the auric boundary's texture and shape. Check the illumination and strength.

Also, how close is it to the object? Does it ebb and flow? Is it closer in some areas than others? How does it feel? Is it hot in some areas? Is it cold in some areas? Practice until you reach a point where you feel completely at ease with what works for you.

Accept you can feel or sense an aura. Use your hands to feel where the energy of a person lies. Is it close? Is it wide? Does it change, or is it constant? Does it flow, or is it sluggish? Practice, practice, practice.

Silence
What is silence? Why is it difficult to find? In our technological age, few places allow us to appreciate the gift of silence, which is truly a gift to the soul.

We are surrounded by and bombarded by sound, most of which goes unnoticed. We have become attuned to white noise and background chatter; it has become a natural part of our day-to-day reality. Even our white goods speak to us: the fridge, the washing machine, the microwave and the list goes on and on.

I never thought I would grow to miss the good things about wash day, soaking whites, scrubbing stains, boiling the copper, more scrubbing, and working the mangle. People did these things to the latest radio songs, laughter, whispered flirtations, or workplace gossip. Oh yes, doing the washing was an experience, not just a job.

It's not a secret that background noise interferes with sleep patterns. Have cars, planes, or loud music ever woken you? It allows an imbalance in our physical, mental, and emotional bodies. It is also the most significant of our cognitive abilities and how we process information. Any background noise can be insidious and controlling.

I am certain most television advertisements use hypnotic language. As consumers, we are unaware of how we are programmed and manipulated. Try turning off the television when not in use and experience the difference in silence. So, try not to watch advertisements. If you do, pull them apart and find the keywords, and you will soon get the true picture.

Reaching silence

Fortunately, options are available to escape the noise drama and give our poor, stimulated brains a long-deserved rest. It is the mother of all things, Mother Nature, in her purest form. Spend time sitting in a natural place—the beach, a park, the bush, or whatever works for you.

Naturally, it needs to be a spot where technology is the last option. Remember, the more people there are, the higher the background noise level. Physically being alone or with others relaxes the mind and de-stresses the body. This is your time to connect with your inner self on a psychic or energetic level and to find the companionship of your soul. It is also a time to connect with the divine within and to allow nature to soothe and heal.

Yes, it may be a tough call; however, the benefits outweigh the effort. Take time to breathe and to still the mind. If thoughts interact, acknowledge them and tell them you will get to them later. Thoughts can be a little like an insistent child; when you are focused on a phone call, they constantly interrupt. Seeking, then demanding attention. If you take a moment to settle the child, fantastic; if not, it's constant chatter.

It's the same thing with thoughts. You assure them you have not forgotten them, and everything is fine. Acknowledging a thought allows you to move forward because you have committed to deal with it. To simplify the process, focus on an object or the words *in* and *out* as you breathe. Accept there is no such thing as absolute silence.

Gypsy Maggie Rose

There are always the sounds of the natural world. The swish of the ocean, the cry screech of the wind, and the howls of a stormy night. There are also birds going about their daily business.

In the bush, you may hear the movement of the wind as it creates songs with the leaves, or tiny sounds of animals or insects, and the buzz of a bee hurrying home with its load of nectar. This is nature, in its purest form, and is a kaleidoscope of sound.

These sounds heal and energise, assist us in releasing our fierce grip on stress, open our eyes to allow tears to wash over pain, and so much more. Turning off the television, radio, phones and computers for a few hours daily will reward you by the bucket load.

Allocate time each day to be silent and observe the shifts in your reality. The lack of noise assists us in hearing more clearly and in releasing anxiety and stress. It also allows us to tune into ourselves and listen to the voice of spirit.

A simple way to connect is to lie on the ground and listen to your heartbeat. In time, you may become aware of the second heartbeat. This is the heartbeat of Mother Earth.

Metaphysical aids

The path between one reality and another is a bit on the tricky side. This is one reason we, mere humans, rely on added help. Not that we cannot reach and bring forth these skills. It is as simple as being a group of people who doubt their abilities and need a support system. Support is diverse, so let's briefly explore some examples. Outside sources activate subconsciously, quietly going about their business while we continue living.

Crystals

Crystals are vibrant, active forces of certain vibrations and retain the energy imparted to them at the point of creation. Crystals have a constant, stable vibration, whereas humans are vibrationally all over the place. Yes, different varieties of crystals carry distinct vibrations, but each is constant. They are healers of the vibration.

They do not move around emotionally like we do, so in a way, they hold sacred space for us. At different times in our lives, we sense a need to either boost or add specific energy, drawing us to particular crystals. Also, the energy can attract more of that vibration into our lives, be it physical, emotional or mental healing.

We should draw love towards ourselves with blessings and financial security or add joy and beauty to our lives and surroundings.

Tarot cards

Tarot is a well-known form of divining the future or understanding a situation. The tarot cards have been around for centuries and have gained power. The symbolism is rich and *speaks* to the soul. The tarot incorporates many things, such as astrology, mysticism, legend, myth and mystery.

The tarot cards link to the subconscious, reminding us of what we know. A tarot card opens doorways for us to explore possibilities anytime, while angel cards inspire and guide us towards a better way of being. Each has its own place and purpose.

Like cards, runes—sometimes small stones bearing symbols of mysterious significance—and other divination methods are vital in understanding everyday issues by tapping into the subconscious. However, they are simply tools. We need to develop an understanding of our personal power and seek help.

Mediumship

Yes, you need to have activated and become attuned to your power to reach beyond the self and allow the connection with other beings. I suggest you do not take this path before you are ready and have learned some pretty advanced protection rites.

You may still pick up messages from loved ones, which could come in many forms, like music, electrical devices doing their own thing, scents and sounds. After all, our loved ones do attempt to make themselves known.

A few years back, I visited Kalgoorlie frequently while travelling. Over time, a client repeatedly enquired about being unable to contact her mother, who had passed over. I repeatedly received the message that Mum was doing her hardest and was being ignored. After four years of drama, my client finally asked me why soup tins are thrown at her in supermarkets.

I thought that was weird until Mum came on board. I asked her what her mum thought about tinned soup. She said her mum hated it and spent many moments telling her to cook a proper meal.

Your connections and links are particular to you, so keep those psychic centres primed. I've had many clients who had *agreed* with loved ones before passing, to wait for a certain word or memory; sometimes it happens, but not always.

The key point is to keep the channels open.

The singing stick
I treated my granddaughters to a meal and a movie, and we discovered the long-lost Mr Fiscus plant in the garden. It brought back clear, wonderful memories. Isn't it strange how we can forget an amazing incident and something mundane shakes it back into our reality?

With the story of Mr Fiscus, I bought this wonderful plant, which sat happily in the lounge until two mother cats had kittens simultaneously. Whoops, they decided, for some unknown reason, that Mr Fiscus was their personal bathroom. I will leave the rest to your imagination. I'm sad to say Mr Fiscus did not survive the trauma. So, having cleared out the sad remains of his home pot, I left it on the porch to dry out. Despite everything, Mr Fiscus still wanted to be part of this world.

He dried out nicely and became a beautiful staff. I had taken him to a few rituals and ceremonies, and he had behaved beautifully; then, it began. During one full moon ceremony, we heard a soft *singing* sound, which was perplexing, as there was no source. An extensive exploration of the area left only one conclusion. Mr Fiscus was *singing*. To say this is unbelievable is a tad on the mild side; I was stunned and decided to sort things out.

Could a beetle or bug have made its home there? I must confess I did not treat said possible beetle with kindness. Into a bath of boiling water, still he sang. I smoked him, still he sang. I gave up and let him *sing* when he had the urge, but always during a ceremony. There was no chance of him being left out.

So, I glued an amazing twin crystal to the top of him for a beach ritual. Standing knee deep in the water—you will not get me any deeper—I cast Mr Fiscus into the ocean. Up he floated, minus the crystal. I opened my hand to the incoming wave, and the crystal was delivered to my hand. I got the message: *keep your crystals to yourself; do not glue stuff on Mr Fiscus*.

He stayed and sang for many years. The interesting thing was that my mum received a cancer diagnosis the week after he started singing. He stopped the week she passed over. After what seemed to be a long time, I burned Mr Fiscus and finally said goodbye to an old friend.

Ouija board

There have been many times in my life where I've denounced the Ouija board as evil. I suppose it was a carryover from my childhood belief system and my occult training. However, my viewpoint has changed slightly after much contemplation and years of doubt.

The Ouija board, or any magical item, is a tool to focus energy. Therefore, it can neither be evil nor good. It is what it is—printed cardboard.

The user's intention is the turning point, and it makes sense when we hear about the skylarking of the young, inquisitive ones. As people perceive it, they approach the game, anticipating being absolutely terrified.

The combination of youth, expectation, alcohol and overactive imaginations can create a scary event. Also, add in the possibility that there could be drugs involved. On the absolute outside, people dealing with puberty could create the right space for poltergeist activity to happen.

Now, I am not saying *do not* or *yeah, go for it.* Treat the experience with respect and prepare yourself and your space. This tool is a conduit for spirit contact, so handle it appropriately. Plus, keep an open mind.

We have come a long way from using the Ouija board, table tapping and other Victorian practices. Used wisely, there is no danger but ensure you have protection in place and that your intentions are open and respectful.

Stepping into spirit

There are so many cards available now that we are spoiled for choice. However, once again, it is about what works for us as individuals. There was a time when I loved the angel cards, but not so much now.

Because we exist in a physical state, these aids act as little light bulb moments in our psychic awareness. In fact, our antenna recognises and reacts to them. Again, different things work for different people. These include crystals, bones, sand drawing, or candle flame in whatever medium or combination gives you an answer is fine and your way.

Emulating someone else may be successful, although it can also be a recipe for disaster. You must be authentic and honest to succeed with any tool. I am unsure whether it was a Confucius, Buddha, or someone different, but the statement that has been my guide is *that when the student is ready, the teacher will come.*

Teachers need not be human; all creatures possess wisdom and lessons to share. Each being must see the lesson and recognise and accept the teacher and teaching when ready.

We enter cycles of growth, and for me, it comes down to an understanding that we are all on a journey—only some are on different planes, trains, and automobiles.

I have broken it down into two pathways that work for me. Feel free to choose and work with your own belief system.

The first pathway is being human, with thinking and working on an Earth-based plan, what you see is pretty much what you get. There may be no connection or need for a spiritual reality. This is fine, as it is how the journey opens for spirit.

The second pathway is spirit crossing over the human experience, where reality is more defined as spirit than human.

Some consider it part of their spiritual journey, and to some extent, it is. However, when we cross that line, there is no turning back—we are changed for all time.

I will outline some steps that will assist you in understanding this crossover. Often, it is a process we are unaware of.

Step 1. You wholly accept that an invisible, incredible force exists within you and all life. You have absolute power, and there is no question about it. The creative force of the universe exists within you. This is a deep, unshakable knowing, not merely a belief.

Step 2. Your thoughts are controlled, shaping your experiences, and creating your reality. You are the creator of your life; no one else but you. The power of thought is what gifts your humanity. Everything about you is held within the power of thought, past, present and future. Your thinking defines your existence.

Step 3. No limitations exist, absolutely none, other than those you impose via *your* thoughts. Reflecting on history, it's incredible that what we now take for granted hadn't *yet* manifested. [Remember that little *yet*.]

Because everything exists, our thoughts are the fuel that makes them reality. Picture a typical home a hundred years ago: no microwave, no washing machine, no vacuum, no indoor plumbing. However, these and many other things already existed elsewhere. We simply needed the mind to bring them forward.

Think about all the so-called miracles in medicine in every walk of life and understand *you* have that same power of creation. What has been achieved once can be repeated. Think about that for a while.

Step 4. Your life has a purpose. Without a doubt, you have a purpose for living and are not seeking aimlessly. You know your purpose is to love and serve humanity in every possible way. You accept your body is a unique, perfectly functioning intelligent system. The invisible bits, like thought and feeling, are a strong part of the essential whole. You are a perfect creation.

Step 5. You accept you can overcome your weaknesses and faults by leaving them behind. Leaving old habits and beliefs behind has roots deep in the invisible realms of your being—the realm of thought. You reach a point where you understand you need to let go or release issues that have become or created obstacles in your day-to-day existence. You may, in fact, remember the issues, and they may try to sneak back in. However, your mind is aware and will notify you to act and change the thought.

Step 6. You will find yourself examining your belief systems and re-assessing what you felt and believed to be impossible. You can and will experience miracles.

Step 7. You can, and do, reach beyond logic, as logic no longer holds you back. Accepting that there are invisible parts of your being that function with you and independently allows the miracle of *you* to unfold. Doors that were jammed tight shut begin to open. Statements that are confounded and confused now make sense. You become less judgemental and more compassionate.

This, my friend, is the next psychic level. Stepping into spirit is not a spirit journey, but a total embracing of your true being.

Chapter Five – Psychic Ability and Spirituality

Psychic ability and spirituality are not necessarily the same, although they have overlapping elements.

A person need not be spiritual to access psychic abilities, nor does one need to access psychic ability to be spiritual. This is a point where we can choose our own path. One is not better than the other; the paths are different.

The entire message of spirituality is outside religion and belief systems—it is a guideline of how to live a good life. Spirituality is your connection and relationship to however you see the creator, God, or by whatever name resonates with you.

Our individual connection to *spirit* is deep and personal. We have no one to make this link for us. Yes, they can guide, direct and open the doorway, but ultimately, it comes down to individual choice.

For me, spirituality exists within and without. It allows us to participate in the union of all things, seen and unseen. For me, the path to spirit is love, and gratitude is the key that opens the doorways.

We have all understood that everything carries a vibration or frequency. We develop and grow as we align with certain frequencies, creating a deeper relationship with spirit.

Many names, including God, goddess, enlightenment, medicine and energy, have known these frequencies through time. These are vibrations we can reach towards, allowing us to reach higher dimensions of learning. In doing so, we receive the blessings associated with these higher energies.

A bit like education, as we accept as normal a brain surgeon, receiving higher rewards than a road sweeper. Everything is in balance with the effort put in. This does not mean one has a lesser ability in the realms of spirit. For example, a beggar and a king are equal in spirit. The soul's education lifts one to higher realms, not an education of the mind.

Spiritual growth comes from the heart and reaches the hearts of others. Belief holds that heart-based thoughts and acts affect the universe. How amazing is that? Each of us can reach beyond our daily reality and influence the universe. What an outstanding joy and responsibility.

Amplifying our connection to the spirit realm increases the flow of love from us and back to us. Ask, and you shall receive. *Yes*, it is a reality. However, to receive, your essence *must* vibrate at the exact frequency of what you wish to attract. Not much love will flow to you if you exist in a constant stream of negative emotions—like attracts like.

If you are constantly miserable, finding fault, angry, and so on, these energies are more likely to enter your space. We need to accept responsibility for our emotional responses to deal with these energies.

All of us encounter times when negative emotions swamp us. Try to avoid being stuck in the cycle. Negative emotions are part of daily life and growth, but we don't need to remain stuck. With the guidance of spirit, we move through them.

Just as we become stuck physically, we can become stuck on emotional levels. Either way, it is our choice to remain stuck or to reach up and move forward.

You are in charge of yourself and your life's direction. Reach for the highest vibe and flow with it; release the resistance and do it.

But how?

Some steps enable you to reach a deep connection with spirit, to your deepest truth.

These steps are:

Step 1. Gratitude: giving thanks for all life has gifted, counting your blessings from the heart, not simply repeating the words—really feel it.

Step 2. Be aware: awareness allows us to immerse ourselves in life's experience and connect deeply to all the surrounding beauty.

Step 3. Relax: take breaks, live in the present, and embrace yourself.

Step 4. Meditation: offers relaxation and connection, and never underestimate the power of contemplation.

Step 5. Breathwork: breath keeps us alive, but there are diverse ways to breathe, consciously aware of ourselves. Aim to become involved in breath work every day.

Step 6. Self-care: looking after your physical, emotional and spiritual needs is the best thing you can do for yourself and your loved ones. Ultimately, we all connect on this incredible journey called life.

Step 7. Being gentle with yourself and others: this is not a race. Remember to laugh, love, share, grow, enjoy, and give thanks for the little things as they create space for bigger things to grow.

To honour spirit is to live in love.

Chapter Six – Chakra System

As every individual has their own aura, so do they have a chakra system. The chakra system is a bit like an added boost, like a protective shield in some ways and a pathway to knowledge in others.

This can become a complicated topic, so I will touch on the basics and allow you to choose further study.

Using your psychic abilities, you can feel, know, and be aware of their activation.

Remember, as no two snowflakes are alike, neither are two humans, so finding your own connections is vital.

What is the chakra system?

What exactly is the chakra system and its importance? Well, yes, it is extremely important. It is a connecting energy system outside the physical body and affects health and well-being on many dimensional levels.

Imagine a flowing, clear and fresh river. That is how energy should flow. However, over time, the river becomes blocked in some areas, by including debris, rubbish, and land changes. So, is our inner river blocked by drama, illness, emotions and the general junk collected from daily living?

There are seven chakra centres, and these are the ones we will focus on first. Then, we will bring in the higher chakra energies. The colour wheel symbolises the basic chakra system, which harmonises with everything. The following paragraphs provide summaries of the chakras.

Root Chakra

The *base* or *root chakra*, at the base of the spine, is represented by the colour red. It relates to the Earth and is associated with our bones, bone marrow and basic cellular health. It also relates to our survival instincts, family and money.

Sacral Chakra

The *sacral chakra* is associated with several glands, including adrenal glands, and is represented by the colour orange. It relates to our emotions and connects us to others, including guilt and negative expression.

Solar Plexus Chakra
The *solar plexus chakra* is associated with the *nervous system* and is represented by the colour yellow. It relates to our mental awareness, coping mechanisms, self-confidence, self-esteem, personal power, and will.

Heart Chakra
The *heart chakra* is associated with lungs and lung tissue and is represented by the colour green. It relates to love, integrity, and compassion, and is our emotional interaction and judgement.

Throat Chakra
The *throat chakra* is associated with our self-expression, intuition and communication, and is represented by the colour blue. It is our truth and understanding of the power associated with optimal body function.

Third Eye Chakra
The *third eye chakra* is associated with skin and brain health at a spiritual level and is represented by the colour indigo. It relates to our inner wisdom and the ability to see beyond the obvious.

Crown Chakra
The *crown chakra* is associated with the connection to your higher self and absolute divinity. It is represented by the colour white.

Sensing Chakra energies

This is a huge area, and we will look at a very simplified version of sensing and balance.

By gently placing your hands on your body and using your psychic senses, you can tune into your energy system and become familiar with your responses.

Crystals can often be the bridge between connections, like a conduit, so if they work for you, use them. Remember, it needs to work for you in your own way. You have a unique system that needs to be treated with care, your way.

For example, if you owned the car of your dreams, house or whatever, you would find out everything about it and treat it with lots of tender, loving care. Your neighbour may have the same item and ignore it, in which case it loses its lustre. Our energy centres are much the same. Connect with them and establish a strong bond to detect imbalances in their cycles, and then you can work with them.

It is a great way to clear, cleanse, and enjoy a functioning chakra system's energy. Like the aura, the chakra collects dust and debris inside and outside our beings; and needs cleaning now and then. The rainbow or chakra diet does that and so much more.

I suggest you start with a day for each chakra centre, aiming for a week each.

Day one: Focus on the *root chakra* and eat foods from the red group—the fresher and purer, the better. It will take some research and should include apples, strawberries, raspberries, rhubarb and radishes. Be inventive; who said a salad could not be? Include strawberries, radicchio, beetroot, capsicum, apple and red wine vinegar. Focus on what the chakra means, and work through family issues. This chakra deals with the bones and marrow, with marrow being a major building block. So, research what feeds the bones. I do not mean to swallow a pill, as this is about proper food equalling real energy.

Day two: Focus on the *sacral chakra* and eat foods from the orange group—the fresher, the better—including oranges, mandarin, peaches, apricots, sweet potato and pumpkin. This chakra is essential to the health of the immune system. It relates to our ability to communicate with others, well-being, sensuality, and sexuality. Work through issues that may be holding you back in this area. *What* stands in the way of your well-being?

Day three: Focus on the *solar plexus chakra and* eat foods from the yellow group—the fresher, the better—including capsicums, peppers, lemons, spices and honey. This chakra relates to our personal power and is the meeting place between the physical and spiritual. It deals with our self-esteem and allows us to grow beyond limits.

Day four: *Wow, this can be a mind-blowing week as things step up from here.* Focus on the *heart chakra* and eat foods from the green group—the fresher, the better—including lettuce, broccoli, sprouts, green apples, plums and pears. In fact, green could be the most abundant food colour. This chakra predominantly deals with matters of the heart, love and self-love, including how we deal with and how we relate to others. A medical condition, *broken heart syndrome*, is a genuine condition, and unfortunately, it can be fatal. The more love in your life, the stronger your immune system.

Day five: Focus on the *throat chakra*, and although this centre can be challenging, eat foods from the blue group, so choosing prunes, blueberries, plums and beetroot, means you are on the right track. Communication is the big issue here. Speaking up for yourself and your truth is tough, but necessary. This chakra can lead to a lot of self-questioning, and once asked, answers are needed.

Day six: Focus on the *third eye chakra*. Although this one can be tricky, it is doable. Try to eat foods from the indigo group, such as eggplant, plums, black garlic, black beans, and grapes. This chakra deals with our intuition and ability to connect with the various centres. It allows us to open to the other senses and the universe.

Day seven: Focus on the *crown* chakra, noting this is a great time to choose, and eat food from the white group, including potato, swede, turnip and mushrooms. This chakra connects us to the divine and our own divinity, with our connection being pure bliss.

Having completed this week of enlightenment, you can expect to be open and aware and maybe a tad over sensitive. So, be gentle with yourself.

Chapter Seven – Infinity Breathing

Keeping good on my promise in *Housekeeping*, we will now discuss on the granddaddy of all breath processes, *infinity breathing*.

Infinity breathing connects you to the consciousness of the creator God. For we are all co-creators in the work of the Universe.

Become very still. Go deeply within. Take some long, slow breaths through the crown chakras. Envision a flow of golden light. Breathe out through the hearth chakra. Envision unconditional love spreading out in a golden haze all around you. With time and practice, this can be expanded to include loved ones and the whole planet.

Now envision before you a golden vibrating infinity symbol connecting from below the earth and reaching into infinite space. Breathe in the golden loop through the chakra at the base of the brain and the top of the spinal cord. Take it down into the Earth. Then, up and breathe out to connect with the loop flowing into the universe.

This is the creative energy source. Use this before manifesting work of any kind.

Now you are able to work with the infinity symbol to activate and increase your energies.

When you are feeling down, tired, nothing left in the tank, take a few minutes to re-group and get the job done.

Process

Relax and breathe gently in whichever way works for you. Just go with what your body tells you.

Standing tall, hold the right arm out to the side. Bringing the arm forward begin *drawing* the infinity symbol in the air (side on figure 8), continue creating this symbol 6 to 10 times. *Change to the left arm.*

Standing tall, hold the left arm out to the side. Bringing the arm forward begin *drawing* the infinity symbol in the air, continue creating this symbol 6 to 10 times.

Hold both arms out in front of the body. With both hands together, begin *drawing* the infinity symbol in the air, continue creating this symbol 6 to 10 times.

Take a few deep breaths and proceed with your day or the work you have in mind.

About the Author

Gypsy Maggie Rose is a 7th generation psychic medium, urban shaman and a leading Australian medium and clairvoyant.

Her grandmother, the great Catherine Mochan, was a gifted healer and herbalist and taught her the ways of the Romani, her people.

Maggie has travelled the world, presenting the popular *Messages from Heaven* event, connecting people with their lost loved ones in spirit. Her gift allows people to find comfort and peace through her readings.

She has featured in Australian television, radio, magazines and the United States media. Maggie has been featured in books by Lucy Cavendish and Jenny

Smedley and in the book *Dying to Know* by Josh Langley, an award-winning Australian author.

Her astounding accuracy and predictions are in high demand, and people worldwide are engaging in discussions about them. Working with some of Australia's most prominent people and overseas celebrities, Maggie assures discretion and privacy to those seeking guidance.

Immerse yourself in the world of Gypsy Maggie Rose and connect with family who have passed over. You can also receive guidance for your own personal journey. Maggie's unbelievable insight and psychic medium abilities will change your life forever.

In this lifetime, Maggie aims to bring the Romani teachings to general use and for the uncertainty to end. In doing so, she will enlighten those who witness it, sharing another Earth tribe's knowledge.

Maggie has been blessed in this living space but knows she carries a two-edged sword.

✦✦✦

https://www.gypsymaggierose.com/

Acknowledgments

I am very blessed in my life to have had many guides on the Earth plane as well as in Spirit.

Pat, who pushed me to step outside my secure area and hit the road.

Fran, who is as weird and wonderful as I am.

Vicky, JJ, and Brigitte are my constant support.

Pauline and Geoff, who have driven me all over the place and introduced me to some amazing spots in this country.

All those who have opened their homes and hearts to light my path on this incredible journey.

Last but not least, Karen, my patient and talented editor.

News and Media

The following media publications and radio stations in Australia and overseas have featured Maggie.

Perth Western Australia Community Newspapers | Advocate | Canning Times | Comment News | Eastern Reporter | Cockburn Gazette | Guardian Express | Hills Gazette | Avon Valley Gazette | Joondalup | Wanneroo Times | Mandurah Coastal Times | Pinjarra Murray Times | Melville Times | Kalamunda Reporter | North Coast Times | Southern Gazette | Stirling Times Weekender | Kwinana Courier | Western Suburbs Weekly | Kimberley Times | Geraldton Guardian: Monthly psychic column | Margaret River Times: Monthly articles | Universal Mind Magazine: monthly channelled readings | Carnarvon Classies: weekly astrology readings | Pashaa Magazine: angel readings.

Radio West Hot FM: Esperance, Kalgoorlie, Merredin, Northam, Katanning, Bunbury, Albany | ABC Radio: Geraldton, Perth | Karratha radio: interviews and footie tipping | Geraldton Spirit Radio: interview and regular appearances | Kyle and Jackie O Show (KIIS 1065) | Triple M Adelaide | Joondalup community radio | Tasmania community radio | Radio West: Ballarat and Wagga Wagga.

Testimonials

Josh Langley, award-winning Australian author
Gypsy Maggie Rose is one of those rare genuine people who makes connecting with the spirit world as natural as breathing. Maggie was instrumental in helping me find evidence that our consciousness continues after we physically die, in my book, Dying to Know: Is there life after death?

Andrew H, client in New Zealand
Maggie is a very gifted lady with very special abilities to give accurate psychic readings and many more services. I have been lucky enough to have had several accurate readings by Maggie over the years while living in Western Australia. Within the readings, Maggie has

information I only know and has been accurate about locations and timeframes.

Sandi Chetwynd, psychic development course participant

After 10 weeks with Maggie, I have to say how much I loved this course. I've learned so much over the weeks; I've become more in tune with my psychic abilities and have grown in my confidence in trusting my feelings/senses. If you are thinking of doing the course, don't hesitate. My time with Maggie has been wonderful; she is wealthy in knowledge, and she knows her stuff! You'll hear glimpses of her magical, wonderful life along the way. I was in awe of everything she spoke about. I'm already missing our weekly lessons, and I hope to learn more from her in the future.

Connect with Maggie

Do you want a psychic or spirit guide reading? Reach out to connect with Maggie. You can also enrol in a psychic development course, shop at the online store, find your horoscope, or sign up for her E-Newsletter.

https://www.gypsymaggierose.com/

https://www.facebook.com/gypsymaggierosepsychic

gypsymaggierose@hotmail.com

www.ingramcontent.com/pod-product-compliance
Lightning Source LLC
Chambersburg PA
CBHW061330040426
42444CB00011B/2847